CEM

MORAL ISSUES IN THE

CW00384368

MORAL ISSUES IN THE HINDU TRADITION

Robert Jackson and Dermot Killingley

tb

Trentham Books

First published in 1991 by Trentham Books

Trentham Books Limited
13/14 Trent Trading Park
Botteslow Street
Stoke-on-Trent
Staffs ST1 3LY

© Robert Jackson and Dermot Killingley 1991

All rights reserved. No part of this publication may be reproduced or transmitted in any form or by any means, electronic or mechanical, including photocopying, recording, or any information storage system, without permission in writing from the publisher.

British Cataloguing in Publication Data
Jackson, Robert
  Moral issues in the Hindu tradition
  1. Religion. Hinduism
  I. Jackson, Robert II. Killingley, Dermot
  I. Title
  294.5

ISBN: 0 948080 50 7

Cover photograph: bride and groom circling the sacred fire at a Hindu wedding in Wellingborough.
Photography: Robert Jackson
Reprinted 1991

Designed by Trentham Print Design and
printed by The Bemrose Press, Chester

Contents

Preface

This book is intended to provide material for teachers who are using GCSE syllabuses in Religious Studies and for students undertaking higher education courses that require some knowledge of Hindu ethics. Many of the topics covered were suggested to the authors by the Southern Examining Group's GCSE syllabus B, 'Personal and social ethics in a religious context'. It is not a class book for pupils, and teachers should exercise discretion in drawing from it. Teaching methods and learning activities for pupils are suggested in R. Jackson and D. Killingley, *Approaches to Hinduism*, London, John Murray, 1988, Chapter 3 and at the end of each of chapters 5-14. These can be drawn on in adapting the material below for use by pupils in class.

Our thanks are due to teachers in Sefton and Warwickshire LEAs and to Stephen Vickers of the University of Oxford Delegacy of Local Examinations for their feedback and encouragement to publish the material. We also thank Babu Govind Garala, Mrs Krishna Garala and Eleanor Nesbitt for their helpful comments and suggestions. Any errors or imbalances are, however, our own. We are grateful to Heather Meldrum for typing the manuscript, and to the University of Oxford Delegacy of Local Examinations for the typesetting.

R.M.D.J.
D.H.K.

Abbreviations

BhG   *Bhagavad-Gītā*

A Sanskrit text in which Krishna instructs his friend Arjuna, and reveals himself as God; included as part of the *Mahābhārata*. Translated in F. Edgerton, *The Bhagavad Gītā* (Harvard University Press, 1972); R.C. Zaehner, *Hindu Scriptures* (Dent, 1966); R.C. Zaehner, *The Bhagavad-Gītā* (Clarendon Press, 1969).

BhP   *Bhāgavata-Purāna* or *Shrīmad Bhāgavatam*

A Sanskrit text composed around the tenth century CE, extolling Krishna and his worship.

Manu   *The Laws of Manu* or *Mānava-Dharma-Shāstra*

A Sanskrit text on law and ritual, composed in the second century CE. Translated by George Bühler (Sacred Books of the East Series, Clarendon Press, 1886).

MBh   *Mahābhārata*

A Sanskrit epic in nearly 100,000 verses, composed over a period between 400 BCE and 400 CE, and containing numerous subsidiary stories and passages of instruction, including the *Bhagavad-Gītā*.

1. Introduction

Hinduism has no 'party line' on morality. Fundamentally, this is because Hinduism is a loosely knit tradition, rather than a religion in the Western sense. Further, the term 'Hindu' (originally the Persian name of the river Indus) was first used by people who were not Hindus, and the term 'Hinduism' did not appear until the early nineteenth century.

Hinduism, then, is not a unity, but a diversity linked by many shared traits. There is no single set of practices, beliefs or behaviour patterns in the Hindu tradition; no single sacred place common to all Hindus; no single source of authority which all Hindus look to. Rather, different Hindus, even in the same place, follow different teachings on practice and belief. Thus it would be a serious error to talk about '*The* Hindu view' on a moral issue. Also, because Hinduism is such an amorphous tradition, it is impossible to draw neat lines between the religious and the social (e.g. over the issue of birth control), or the religious and the superstitious – though individual Hindus make their own distinctions.

With Hinduism, perhaps more than with other religions, it would be misleading to present one set of views as the religion's stance on the ethical issues listed in the syllabus. If we took one set of texts – say the hymns of the Rig-Veda, or the Laws of Manu, or one of the more popular texts such as Tulsī Dās' epic of Rāma – or if we took one teacher such as Vivekānanda or Gāndhi, or the practices of one group of Hindus such as the Swāminārāyanīs, we might find a coherent set of answers to some, although not all, of the questions raised; but that set of answers would not be the Hindu stance, because different answers could be found elsewhere in the historical and social spread of Hinduism. All we can do is to exemplify; and it is a matter for debate whether the examples we choose are typical or not. Since the *Bhagavad-Gītā* is easily available, and embodies many important Hindu ideas, we will take some examples from it, but we will also look at other sources, ancient and modern, and at what some Hindus actually do in practice.

Examination syllabuses require that we concentrate on the shared traits. But we must constantly remember that these traits only tell part of the story. Never use the expression 'All Hindus ...'. There are exceptions to every generalisation. Within the Hindu tradition there are different and sometimes conflicting views of what Hinduism – or the 'real' or 'true' Hinduism – is. For this reason it is important to have an overview of the tradition before going to particular examples of writing on Hindu ethics, sources which report Hindu views on moral questions, or Hindu guest speakers. Individual views can then be set in the context of the Hindu tradition.[1]

The distinctiveness of Hinduism

Despite all the diversity, there are some general *tendencies* of belief and practice within the Hindu tradition that gave it a distinctive flavour – though no single belief or practice is universal. Some of these – ones that are relevant to Hindu ethics – are introduced below.

1. Time

One tendency is a view of time in the long term that puts our immediate concerns with time into perspective. Our year is but a day to the gods. The gods' year is 360 of ours. 12,000 years of the gods make up *one* cycle of four ages (yugas). In the first of these four ages the world is perfect, but in each succeeding age it declines: lives are shorter, food is scarcer and morality lower. We are now in the worst age (*kali yuga*), which began with the great battle described in the Mahābhārata in 3,102 BCE, and it will end when Kalki, the tenth avatāra of Vishnu, comes to punish the wicked and begin a new perfect age.[2] According to the above scheme, this will not happen for over 4,000 centuries. For the forseeable future, we live in a far from perfect world, and moral judgements must take this into account.

2. God, selves and nature

Another general tendency is the idea that all existence can be summed up in the terms God, selves and nature. In one school of Indian philosophy, called Advaita Vedānta, the distinction between these terms is ultimately false; but they are useful nevertheless in describing the illusory world in which we find ourselves. (Advaita Vedānta philosophy has been influential in this century and underpins the teachings of the Rāmakrishna Mission and its Vedānta centres.)

God can be thought of as an impersonal absolute (Brahman), or as a personal deity (e.g. Vishnu, Shiva, Shakti). Hindu philosophies have different views on whether God is the substance out of which the world is made or whether nature is eternally separate from God. (The Ramakrishna Mission, following the medieval philosopher Shankara, would take the first view; ISKCON – the International Society for Krishna Consciousness or Hare Krishna movement – would hold that the question cannot be rationally answered.)

The self (*ātman*) is eternal and changeless and does not undergo birth or death. It is involved in the round of birth and death through connection with a body. Even away from the physical body, the self is restricted by the subtle body or personality, which includes the intellect and the mind among other faculties. The intellect can learn to control the sense faculties and the action faculties (e.g. speech, movement, reproduction) through the mind. This discipline or control is called yoga. This kind of view influences the Sathya Sai Baba organisation's educational material, for example. This material teaches that, through developing the memory and the intuition (e.g. by 'silent sitting'), the individual can realise the soul, 'the resident divinity in each person and object'.

2

Nature consists of three strands (*guna*) which combine in various proportions to produce the characters of different people and a variety of phenomena. The view strongly influences Hindu views about diet. Members of ISKCON, for example, specify that members should eat foods in which the strand of *sattva* or goodness is predominant and should avoid foods with the quality of *rajas*, which influence the passions, or of *tamas*, which induce lethargy and laziness; such a diet would require abstinence from meat-eating. There are further reasons for avoiding killing animals, summed up in the term *ahimsā*, non-violence; many Hindu groups, though by no means all, are vegetarian.[3]

3. Dharma and karma

Dharma and *karma* are key terms in discussing moral questions. *Dharma* is a rich concept which can be roughly equivalent to 'duty' or 'obligation'. It can also mean 'natural function' (the *dharma* of fire is to burn), or 'way of life'; it is often used to translate 'religion', and Hindus speak of the 'Hindu dharma'. By following one's *dharma* one is living correctly, and thereby accumulating merit.

One's actions are held to affect one's destiny in the future. By doing good actions – that is, actions according to one's *dharma* – one gets good fortune in this life and also in future births, and by evil action one gets evil fortune. The word *karma* refers both to actions and to the fortune which results from them.

An individual's *dharma* comprises the moral obligations towards family and the wider community, including non-human beings, which automatically follow from being born with a particular sex and in a particular family and caste, and from relationships entered into during life. *Dharma* is relative, in that a wife's *dharma* will be different from her husband's, a young man's different from an old man's, and a sweeper's different from a brahmin's. There can also be situations of moral conflict. The *Bhagavad-Gītā*, for instance, starts from Arjuna's dilemma in which he feels an obligation to his kinsmen, though in the end he fights them because of his overriding *dharma* as a *kshatriya*, a member of the warrior class.[4]

4. Caste, purity and pollution

A caste is a group of people who are considered to be related to each other, usually claiming a legendary common ancestor. Caste members also often share a traditional occupation (which may or may not still be practised). Caste is hereditary and, with few exceptions, marriage is within the caste (i.e. castes are normally endogamous). Castes have a regional base, though their members may migrate. Castes are ranked (by other castes) according to the degree of ritual purity or pollution associated with their traditional occupation, whether or not they continue to practise it. What is relevant is *ritual* purity and polution, not *moral* goodness or superiority. Once born into a caste, you remain a member of it for life regardless of your economic or political status.

Caste permeates South Asian life and exists in religious groups in India that are not Hindu (e.g. Muslims, Christians, Sikhs). The word 'caste' is derived from the Portuguese *casta*, meaning 'lineage' or 'breed'; the most common Indian word is *jāti*, meaning 'birth'. Caste should not be confused with *varna*, the four traditional divisions of Indian society. While there are hundreds of castes, there are only four varnas: brahmins (the priestly class), kshatriyas (warriors and rulers), vaishyas (cultivators and traders) and shūdras (who serve the other three varnas). This fourfold social order is important in Hindu texts on *dharma*, but does not match the actual divisions of Hindu society.

Generally a caste ranks higher the more castes will accept drinking water or cooked food from it. Brahmin castes are ranked at the top and untouchable castes at the bottom. The ranking order between these two groups is often disputed. Priesthood is the traditional occupation of male brahmins, though only a minority operate as priests.

Villages account for about 80 per cent of India's population, and a village may include as many as twenty or as few as two castes. The caste that turns out to be economically and numerically dominant may by no means be the highest in terms of ritual purity.

The *Laws of Manu* (a Smriti – 'remembered' – text from the second century CE) gives details for avoiding and removing pollution. Ordinary Hindus do not learn from such texts, however, but in the home from the mother and other older members of the family, and later from local elders. Pollution is involved in all bodily functions: excretion (after which one washes carefully using the left hand); perspiration (hence the dhobi – washerman – castes are low); cutting of hair and nails (hence barber castes are low); menstruation (e.g. menstruating women do not enter the kitchen or the temple); birth (which is both polluting and dangerous; the mother, child and family have to go through purification rituals after a birth); death (when pollution is acquired through proximity to the deceased, and also through kinship).

Anyone can be polluted temporarily. Members of impure castes are, however, permanently polluted, by virtue of being born into the caste. Several ritual actions are capable of removing temporary pollution, including: bathing in running water (e.g. in a river; pouring water over oneself); drinking water from a sacred river; exposure to the sun; touching a cow.

Although caste distinctions need to be understood in ritual terms, it is inevitable that caste will be discussed as a moral issue. The first thing to say is that the Hindu tradition is far less individualistic than western Christian tradition. In India both the family and the caste are networks of mutually responsible people. This collectivism can have advantages, especially in Indian village life. There is solidarity between members of the same caste, which overrides differences of wealth, so that the poor can be respected and helped by caste fellows. Since occupations are partly determined by caste, skills and equipment can be passed on through generations. Village life involves a system of exchange of goods and services between castes, which helps to distribute resources and employment opportunities. Caste also helps groups of very different culture to co-exist symbiotically in the village.

Urban life and migration have brought about significant modifications to the caste system, which is in a state of perpetual adaptation, though it shows no signs of disappearing. The most commonly criticised aspect of the system, both from inside as well as outside the Hindu tradition, is untouchability. Many Hindus would agree with the Hindu philosopher T.M.P. Mahadevan that 'Untouchability is the greatest blot on Hinduism'. Although a few untouchables have risen economically or politically, most are amongst the poorest and most exploited people in India. Their situation is discussed further in Chapter 3.

The journey through life

Hindus believe that our present life is only one among countless lives, in which each of us is repeatedly born and repeatedly dies. The form in which we are born depends on our previous karma. There are a number of perspectives on a person's journey through life that are relevant to Hindu ethics. These are the four stages of life, the four aims or goals of life and the three ways to salvation. They should be seen as ideals which influence thinking and behaviour, rather than as systems of belief and action which are closely followed.

1.   The four stages of life

According to tradition, a man's life, apart from childhood, passes through four stages, called *āshramas* (the same word also means a place where ascetics live). (This pattern traditionally applies to 'twice-born' castes, those associated with the top three *varnas*). First he becomes a *brahmachāri*, an ascetic student studying the Vedas under a guru. Next comes the stage of the householder (*grihastha*), into which he is initiated at marriage; here he provides for his family materially, conducts rituals, and raises children. The third stage, which he can only enter when his line of descent has been secured by his son begetting a son, is that of the forest hermit (*vānaprastha*). Finally comes the *sannyāsī*, who has renounced all ties and no longer performs any ritual. The stage of vānaprastha is generally obsolete, and quite early texts claim that one can become a sannyāsī at any time without going through the other stages; this is frequently done. Nevertheless the pattern of preparation for adult life, followed by active and prosperous married life, and finally by withdrawal from the world, is a powerful ideal for Hindus. The traditional pattern for a woman's life is simpler. She passes straight from childhood to marriage, and if widowed is expected to lead an ascetic life.

5

2. The four aims

A person has three aims in this world: the lowest is *kāma*, meaning pleasure, the satisfaction of desires; next is *artha*, wealth and worldly power, and above that is *dharma*, the fulfilment of one's duties as determined by caste, stage of life and other factors. All these aims are legitimate, but the lower must be subordinated to the higher, so that one does not lose one's wealth in pursuit of pleasure, or gain power wrongfully. Much of a Hindu's behaviour, like anyone else's, can be accounted for by these three aims; this applies to religious as well as other behaviour.

Overriding these three worldly aims is the transcendent aim of *moksha* – salvation, release from rebirth. The state is described differently by different schools, though it always includes freedom from the bondage resulting from one's previous deeds. For most people moksha is a remote aim, only to be reached in their present life by those who have formed an aversion to worldly things and become ascetics (*sannyāsīs*), or by ardent devotees.

3. The three ways (mārga)

Modern expositions of Hinduism often refer to a set of three ways to salvation (or three yogas or disciplines): the way of action (*karma-mārga*), the way of devotion (*bhakti-mārga*), and the way of knowledge (jnāna-mārga). Older accounts of the way of action refer principally to ritual action. Modern thinkers, however, stress public service rather than ritual action in their interpretation of *karmamārga*. Often the three ways are regarded as separate paths to the same goal for people of different temperaments.

Sects and movements

Although it is impossible to say unequivocally what 'the' Hindu view is on a moral question, it *is* possible to state the moral views of particular sects and movements within the Hindu tradition. For many centuries such movements have brought vitality to the tradition, and have often acted as mediators of philosophical ideas to ordinary people. Today, in Britain as well as India, they provide many Hindus with explicit codes of belief and conduct to guide them through the perplexities of the modern world. They use books, magazines, comic strips, public speaking, air travel and videos to reach a far wider audience than in earlier times.

Vaishnavas, Shaivas and Shaktas (worshippers of Vishnu, Shiva and Shakti) are sometimes called sects. But within each of these broad bands there are widely differing beliefs and practices. Each of the sects and movements we are thinking about consists of a group of people following a distinct set of doctrines and practices, and looking to a particular person (living or dead) as their teacher, as their authority in the interpretation of tradition, as a way to God, or as a manifestation of God. The term *sampradāya* ('handing on'; 'tradition') is sometimes used of such movements. Through the gurus of a *sampradāya*, members of a sect are linked to its founder and learn its beliefs and practices.

In some groups the authority of the sect lies in the founder's charisma, in others in his ability to give reliable expositions of received teachings. Some founders have both qualities.

The nineteenth century saw the foundation of many movements which sought to preserve the best in the Hindu tradition while using modern ideas and methods. The first of these was the Brāhmo Samāj, founded in Calcutta in 1828, which pioneered some important social reforms. Others are the Ārya Samāj, founded in Bombay in 1875 but flourishing mainly in the Punjab, and the Rāmakrishna Mission, named after the charismatic teacher Rāmakrishna, but developed doctrinally by Swami Vivekānanda on the basis of the Vedānta philosophy[5]. Many of the ideas and social norms promoted by such movements have since become the common property of modern Hindus.

Several sects and movements thrive among Hindu communities in Britain. These include the Pushti Mārga, a distinctively Gujarati sect, with members principally from the Lohāna caste; the Ārya Samāj, which has many Punjabi members; The Rāmakrishna Mission; ISKCON, the Hare Krishna movement, with a substantial western and a growing ethnically Indian following, founded in 1965 but traceable back to the charismatic teacher Chaitanya;[6] and the Sathya Sāi Bābā organisation, a rapidly growing movement. Its founder, Sathya Sāi Bābā (born in 1926 and still living), is believed by his followers to be divine – an *avatāra* (descent) of Shiva and his wife Shakti, and of other deities such as Vishnu.

Some of these movements produce educational material which gives an authentic view of Hindu beliefs and values as seen by the movement, though not necessarily by all Hindus. ISKCON publishes a wide range of books for adults and children, and also posters. Like other movements dedicated to the worship of Krishna it emphasizes non-violence in general and vegetarianism in particular; it publishes a richly illustrated collection of Indian vegetarian recipes, with an introduction stating the movement's position on vegetarianism with reference to economic and health issues as well as to Hindu scriptures.[7] The Sathya Sai Baba movement is committed to promoting the values of Truth, Righteous Conduct, Peace, Love and Non-Violence. These values are explored and taught at classes for children organised by the movement in several British towns and cities under the title Bāl Vikās (child blossoming), and by the Society for Education in Human Values, which is part of the movement.[8]

Teaching about moral issues in Hinduism

There is no problem, in terms of balance and sources of authority, in teaching the moral views of particular Hindu sects and movements. It is when an attempt is made to give a general Hindu view that distortion is likely. In the case of most

7

of the issues covered by examination syllabuses there is no single Hindu view. Further, over some issues it is very difficult, if not impossible, to separate distinctively religious views from wider social views. There is also a problem over sources of authority. The Vedic spirit is influential, but it would be a mistake to equate Hindu moral views with prescriptions in the classical texts. It has to be remembered that much Hindu tradition is transmitted orally and by custom, especially through women in the family, whose collective memory is sometimes called the fifth Veda. Hindu scriptures are not normally read in the same way that Protestant Christians read and use the Bible. The *Bhagavad-Gītā* has achieved its popularity only within the last hundred years, and the interpretations of its teachings are as varied as its interpreters. Gandhi is sometimes taken as a representative Hindu, but his views are very individual, and influenced by his experience outside India. He did not read the Gītā until he was 21, and even then he read it in English. Like many Hindus, however, he was familiar with popular versions of certain traditional myths.[9] Such stories, traditionally remembered and told by grandmothers and mothers, and now often found in children's comic books or as the subject matter of films on video-cassette, still have an important function in the transmission of traditional values. Some stories are linked to religious festivals, and so provide an annual reminder of religious values.

A problem for non-Hindu students is a tendency to superimpose their own moral categories and beliefs on to Hinduism without first grasping the relevant key concepts and social structures from the Hindu tradition. An empathy game, designed to raise students' awareness of this tendency, is found in Jackson and Killingley (1988) Chapter 3, pp 24-25. Other activities and methods which may help in designing teaching material are to be found in the same chapter and at the end of chapters 5-14.

Notes

1. See further R. Jackson and D. Killingley, *Approaches to Hinduism* (John Murray, 1988), Chapter 2. This book includes much material relevant to a study of Hindu moral belief and practice.

2. See *Dasha Avatar*, p. 87. *Dasha Avatar* (Ten Avatars) is one of a popular children's series in comic book form, *Amar Chitra Katha*, published in India and available from Asian bookshops and general stores.

3. Jackson and Killingley, *Approaches to Hinduism*, pp 36-39; 194.

4. See *Bhagavad-Gītā*, Chapter 1, verse 26 – Chapter 2, verse 38. For further ideas about dharma, see Jackson and Killingley, *Approaches to Hinduism*, pp 16, 68, 76-86.

5. Publications of the Ramakrishna Mission are available from the Ramakrishna Vedanta Centre, Blind Lane, Bourne End, Bucks, SL8 5LG.

6. Kim Knott's *My Sweet Lord* (Aquarian Press, 1986) places ISKCON in its wider Hindu context.

7. Adiraja dasa, *The Hare Krishna Book of Vegetarian Cooking*. This and other publications are available from the Bhaktivedanta Book Trust, Croome House, Sandown Road, Watford, Herts. WD2 4XA.

8. The following texts used in Bāl Vikās (child blossoming) classes are published by the Sri Sathya Sai Bal Vikas Education Trust, Prasanthi Nilayam, India: a booklet, *Curriculum and Methodology for Integrating Human Values in Education* (international edition) and *Teacher's Handbook for the Course in Human Values* are written for teachers, while *Education in Human Values*: Primer I, II, *Pathfinder*, I, II and *Stories for Children* I, II are produced for pupils. These texts are not available through booksellers but are available from some Sathya Sai Baba groups (e.g. Sri Sathya Sai Centre of Wembley, 35 Clifton Avenue, Middlesex). The monthly newspaper, the *Sai World Gazette*, is another useful source of material (from the Editor, Devereux House, 50 Longley Road, London, SW17 9LL).

9. See Jackson and Killingley, *Approaches to Hinduism*, pp 154-7.

2. The family and marriage

The account that follows principally uses members of Hindu communities and anthropological reports as sources. As such it is partial and anecdotal and it covers a limited range of ethnicities, castes and age-groups. No statement should be taken as representing 'the Hindu point of view'.

Hindu families

Generally speaking, the family is the joint family, usually a number of brothers and their wives and children, and the brothers' parents. The sons of one father will not all necesarily live with him at the same time, but some of them are likely to do so some of the time. Even where the joint family does not share a house, it shares wealth to some extent; for instance, men working away from home may send money to their fathers, or – if the father is not alive – to their eldest brothers, and conversely fathers provide capital to set up their sons in business or to train them. Prestige is also shared, and *ijjat* or *izzat* – family honour – is of crucial importance. Any bad behaviour by an individual brings disgrace on the whole family. Respect for elders, both male and female, is a key value.

Hindu children, like other children of Asian origin, grow up with a strong sense of the importance of family relationships. In fact they are encouraged to address all relatives not by name or by name only but with a word indicating relationship, for example, Aunty Kamla will be Aunty, Kamla Aunty or Auntyji ('jī' is a suffix which shows respect). For Aunty (if the English word is not used) there will be a different word to show whether the aunt is the mother's sister (mausī), the mother's brother's wife (māmī), the father's sister (buā), the father's younger brother's wife (chāchī), or the father's older brother's wife (tāi). These are the Hindi terms, but each Indian language has its own range of words to indicate these relationships.

This may seem very complicated, but it does remove a good deal of confusion. In English it is not clear whether 'granny' is someone's father's mother or mother's mother, let alone whether 'uncle' is mother's brother, father's sister's husband, etc. Particularly in homes and communities where relations are constantly together or meeting frequently it helps to know exactly who is who. Having many different names for different types of uncle, aunt, etc. is not only an Asian custom. In ancient Greece, too, there were more words than we have in English. Notably it is usual in all societies where people tend to live together in joint families.

A Hindu child is brought up to feel as closely bonded to cousins as to siblings. Nobody addresses or refers to a cousin as cousin but always as brother or sister. In English too Hindus will speak like this, feeling that the English terms are too cold and distant. Your cousin really is your brother or sister. So you may hear someone say 'I saw my brother's father', i.e. my uncle. To make a distinction, if questioned, people will distinguish between 'real brothers (or sisters)' and 'cousin brothers (or sisters)'. Parents feel hurt by their children's lack of respectful affection if they refer to their parents' friends as 'Mr X' or 'Shāntā'. Instead the children are expected to say 'uncle', 'Bābu uncle' or 'aunty', 'Shāntā Mausī', 'Mausījī' etc. In Gujarati, the language spoken by most of Britain's Hindu population, many first names have the suffixes bhāī (brother) or ben (sister) e.g. Lalubhāī, Savitriben. The full name (i.e. with suffix) would be used by contemporaries.

In Hindu families in Britain it is usual for a woman to live with her husband in his parents' house for several years after marriage. Many Hindu families have bought adjacent terraced houses or very large detached houses, so that children here often grow up with their cousins, their father's brother's families, their father's unmarried sisters and his parents. On the other hand, it is not a Hindu custom for a girl's parents to live with her after marriage, nor would a man's married sisters and their children share his household.

At weekends and during holidays British Hindu children are likely to spend more time going to weddings (attended by many relatives), watching videos of their relations' weddings, and visiting relations' houses in other cities, than non-Asian children do. Festivals also reinforce relationships, especially Raksha Bandhan, in August, when sisters tie rākhis, 'bracelets' (often made of wool and tinsel) on the wrists of their brothers. The brother-sister tie is one of the most sacred and abiding, and a girl who has no brother is felt to be most unfortunate. Fasts also reinforce relationships – for instance, wives fast for their husbands' welfare on Karwa Chauth (in October), or for their daughters at other times.[1]

Seema's family

Seema is an eleven year old Hindu girl who speaks Hindi to her family. The family tree shows the words she would use in addressing her parents, uncles and aunts, and grandparents. The suffix 'jī' is added to each term because this is the way in which affectionate respect would be shown. Seema's mother would not call Seema's mausī 'mausī' but would use the word 'bahin' (i.e. sister).

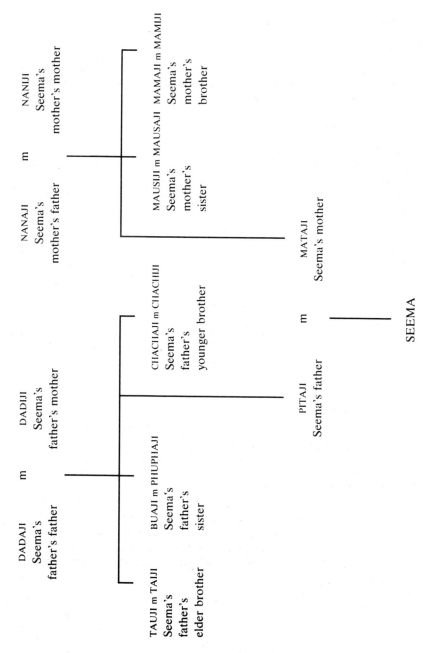

Marriage

1. Hindu marriage law

There are different sources of legal authority in Hindu India: customary law; Brahmanical or Sanskritic law; and national law. For Hindus living in Britain, there is also British law to consider.

(a) Customary law

Hindus in Gujarat, Tamil Nadu, the Punjab or West Bengal may be governed by totally different customary rules, but all are referred to as 'Hindu law'. Thus traditional Hindu law is highly localized, and in the case of marriage the position of the individual Hindu as a member of a particular family, clan or caste will determine how a marriage is solemnized, and what obligations it involves.

(b) Brahmanical or Sanskritic law

This is based on an enormous variety of Sanskrit sources written by Brahmins; some of these are now lost. Surviving texts tend to differ in points of detail over the various rites that make up a complete marriage ritual. The *Laws of Manu* (or *Manusmriti*) says virtually nothing about the ritual details of marriage ceremonies, but does lay down that the legal validity of the marriage is indicated by the completion of the *saptapadī*, a ritual involving taking seven steps around (or before) a sacred fire. This ritual is not mentioned in all the relevant texts. Marriage, according to the Brahmanical texts, is one of the *samskāras*, 'sacraments' or rites of passage.

(c) National law

There was no unified Indian national marriage law for Hindus until the Indian Parliament passed the Hindu Marriage Act of 1955. The Act allows that any customary form of Hindu marriage ceremony leads to a lawful union.

Section 7 of the Act reads:

> A Hindu marriage may be solemnized in accordance with the customary rites and ceremonies of either party thereto. Where such rites and ceremonies include the saptapadī (that is, the taking of seven steps by the bridegroom and the bride jointly before the sacred fire), the marriage becomes complete and binding when the seventh step is taken.

14

Section 3 of the Act defines 'customary':

> The expressions 'custom' and 'usage' signify any rule which, having been continuously and uniformly observed for a long time, has obtained the force of law among Hindus in any local area, tribe, community, group or family: Provided that the rule is certain and not unreasonable or opposed to public policy; and provided further that in the case of a rule applicable only to a family it has not been discontinued by the family.

This rule allows great latitude to Hindu brides, grooms and parents, but has created many problems for courts in view of the difficulty of deciding what, in a particular case, is a valid custom.[2]

(d) British law

When a Hindu couple marry in England or Wales, they have to apply for a licence from a registrar and go through a ceremony in a register office. This ceremony is not regarded as religiously valid by Hindu communities, however, and a Hindu wedding will be held at a later date, often in a day or two. In the meantime the couple would live in their respective homes and the marriage would not be consummated. The Hindu wedding might be in a temple, a community building or a hall hired for the occasion.

2. Partner selection

Marriage is between families, rather than individuals. It is monogamous and normally is within the caste. Partners must not be too closely related and, although there are many variations, it can be taken as a rule of thumb for North India that you must not marry someone with a common grandparent. Thus, in contrast to English law, a North Indian Hindu is not permitted to marry a first cousin. When young people reach marriageable age, both sets of parents keep their eyes open for a suitable match, though who makes the first move varies according to caste tradition. Traditionally a particular person – a friend or a relative – would have acted as a go-between. Among migrant communities marriage bureaux are common (one community leader runs a non profit-making bureau as a social service) and contacts can be made across several national boundaries. Advertisements appear in the press in India, and in the Indian press here. The *Indian Express*, for example, often includes Christian and Sikh as well as Hindu advertisements – showing that arranged marriage is a South Asian and not specifically a Hindu phenomenon. Such advertisements frequently show the importance of caste, of educational qualifications and of appearance (e.g. of fair or 'wheatish' complexion in girls). Other factors include age, temperament, vegetarianism and non-smoking. Some advertisements say 'no caste bar' or 'caste immaterial'. Not mentioned, but understood, are questions of relative wealth – e.g. owning land and property.

Though the system of arranged marriage is maintained outside India, it is subject to a degree of liberalisation, and occasionally young people break out of the system. Amongst middle class professional society in urban India, for at least two generations, there have been fairly liberal attitudes towards marriage, so one should not conclude that liberalisation is only associated with residence outside India.

The following extract is from a booklet[3] which gives an indication of current attitudes and practices within one Gujarati Hindu community in Britain. The writers recognise the influence of western individualism on young people, especially through education, and predict a certain degree of liberalisation within the Gujarati community. Nevertheless they counsel caution:

> What the Indian girl's parents worry about is letting her have her way now, letting her marry the man she loves, being rejected by her family (including them) and then later in life if widowed or divorced she will have nothing to fall back on. Widows and divorcees who have 'kept to the rules' are cared for by the family and community. However, this modern girl will have no-one to care for her, and so the parents wish to prevent those circumstances arising by making her realise, or if necessary (in a few cases only) forcing on her, the importance of 'keeping to the rules'.

Another useful source is Amarjit Khera's 'The Status of Women in Hindu Society'.[4] Ms Khera writes as a Punjabi woman and as a Community Relations Officer working in Southall. The following passage records some of her observations about arranged marriage in Southall that reveal some flexibility in the system.

> Marriages are still arranged, to a large extent ... Yet in the majority of cases the girls have a lot of say in the matter and they do not just have the choice of looking at one man, but they will have half-a-dozen or more to consider ... Many girls want to have an arranged marriage. Because they are not going to clubs, they are not in a position in which they meet men whom they might marry ... They accept the arrangements of their fathers or of their family elders, whereby they introduce the boys to them, and I think the girls are getting a good deal here ... A brother of the girl may make inquiries about how the prospective bridegroom has behaved in this situation or in that. Naturally there is a kind of assessment that is undertaken by the family before they bring the boy to the girl but then the girl has the final say, and many say, 'Sorry, I do not want to marry you. I do not like you for this reason or that reason.' ... But, of course, there are exceptional cases where a girl is forced to marry against her will.

3. Betrothal

Betrothal ceremonies vary between castes and from region to region. A Gujarati brahmin woman informant reported that betrothal is a religious ceremony involving a brahmin priest and both the boy and girl. The couple meet in the same hall with the boy's party on one side and the girl's on the other. This woman had not heard of engagements in which couples did not meet. A Gujarati goldsmith woman, on the other hand, reported separate engagement ceremonies, one in India and one in Britain, involving an exchange of gifts, with the bride-to-be's family sending a gift to the future groom and vice versa.

This particular woman had her engagement 18 months before marrying. She received a *chunri* (head covering) and a sari from the boy's family, and sweets, a coconut and some items of jewellery – a gold chain, gold bangles and a nose stud. Wearing a sari, she had to sit on a chair and her future husband's cousin draped a red and green sari over her head so that the *pallu* (the decorative end) hung over her head and she held the rest in her lap. Her fiancé was still in India and she thinks that he had a similiar ceremony there. She says that some couples from her community now have this ceremony early on the day of the wedding.

4. Dowry

In India dowry (*dahej* in Hindi) is against the law (Dowry Prohibition Act 1961), and objections to it have been part of many Hindu social reform movements. Nevertheless the customary practice of giving a daughter sufficient wealth on marriage to prevent her being criticised by her in-laws is widely, though not universally, followed. Though there is great variety among castes, traditional items taken into her new family by the bride included gold, jewellery and quantities of saris. These days items might include a refrigerator, a television set, furniture or a car. Another way the practice operates in the UK is that working girls save their wages and take the accumulated sum with them into the marriage, perhaps as a down-payment on a mortgage. Ramaben Patel's personal view of British Gujarati practice is as follows:

> Here in the UK one still finds families practising this system. A girl and her parents have no other alternative but to submit to the other party's demands if they wish to acknowledge or accept the ties of marriage between their daughter and the boy. In many families these days the sons themselves take a firm hold on the situation and refuse to marry according to the Hindu traditional ceremony if there is going to be any dowry bargain – but he would still proclaim to marry the girl at a Registrar's Office. One could only wish that every young man would help in eliminating this system, as they can do this best, but it seems to work only very slowly. With any luck probably in a couple of decades or so it might have disappeared.[5]

5. Wedding rituals

Given the flexibility of Indian law on marriages there is an immense variety of ritual activity in Hindu wedding ceremonies. The *saptapadī* (seven steps) is not universal in customary law, and is not essential according to national law except where it is customary, yet many Indian law cases have ruled that it is essential. In the ancient version of *saptapadī* the bride and groom would take seven steps, either east or north. Before that the couple would walk four times round the fire which was the centre of the ritual. In modern times these two stages of the ritual may still be performed, as shown in the slide set *A Hindu Wedding*.[6] Often, however, the two stages are combined, either by circling the fire seven times, or by making four circles of seven steps each.

The steps are often marked with a row of seven areca nuts; the bride steps from one nut to the next while the priest tells the significance of each step. The first is for food, the second for strength, the third for wealth, the fourth for happiness, the fifth for cattle, and the sixth for the seasons. At the seventh step, the two are joined in friendship. Since most Hindus nowadays do not keep cattle, the fifth step may be understood as signifying children.

Patel and Lambert (see note 3) do not mention the *saptapadī*, but say that the circumambulation ceremony 'solidifies their marriage and makes them husband and wife', while each circumambulation signifies one of the four stages of human life.

> During the first three rounds the groom is in the front, the bride following, signifying 'I shall follow you wherever you go – in happiness or in hard times'. On the final round, the bride goes in front and the groom follows. This signifies that during old age, when the time for departing comes, the woman makes her wishes ... to die first, and not be left behind as a widow.

The *saptapadī* issue illustrates that it is impossible to give a precise summary of the wedding ceremony. Both the content and order of events can vary greatly, though a common feature of the ritual is an increase in contact between the bride and groom as the ceremony progresses, marking their approaching unity. In the slide set *A Hindu Wedding* (note 6) the bride and groom are initially separated by a veil; then they garland each other; they are tied together; they hold hands (first under the veil, then publicly); they sit side by side and perform several joint rituals involving public touching (making offerings, circum-ambulations, the saptapadī) culminating in feeding each other.

6. Widowhood, divorce and remarriage

In Hindu terms, a wife can only have one husband in her present lifetime, though a man is permitted to remarry. A widow remains dependent on her husband's family, and is traditionally expected to lead an ascetic life, wearing plain clothes, usually a white sari, and without the jewellery worn by a married woman. However, some widows do remarry, and Hindu reform movements such as the Brahmo Samaj have campaigned for widow remarriage. In the UK, friends sometimes take the place of the family in supporting young widows.

As an alternative to widowhood, some women have chosen to die on the funeral pyres of their husbands. Such a woman is called a *satī* ('true woman'), and is believed by some to achieve great benefits for herself and for her husband, and for those who worship at the monument commemorating her. The word *satī*, spelt in the old-fashioned English way *suttee*, was applied by the British to the practice, but properly it refers to the woman herself. The practice was forbidden by law in British India in 1829, and this prohibition is continued in present-day India. Nevertheless, there have been occasional occurrences, including a celebrated one in Rajasthan in 1987, which caused a storm in the Indian press lasting several months. This practice, which has never been common, is an extreme expression of the wife's lifelong devotion to her husband.

Indian national law permits divorce, but there are strong community pressures against it. As one Punjabi wife in her late 20s and living in England puts it, 'The sort of girl who gets divorced can probably stand up for herself'. This is not so likely to be the case if it is the husband who initiates the divorce. A divorced woman usually returns to her parents or brother, and a second marriage is arranged for her if possible. When a woman remarries, whether as a widow or after divorce, the Hindu marriage ritual is often shortened, or omitted altogether. One Gujarati woman (of the goldsmith caste and resident in England) reports that in her experience, after the death of a spouse or a divorce a man usually remarries, but a woman does not. Whether the woman stays with her in-laws or her parents depends on the circumstances. If she has children, her job is to look after them.

Adoption and the care of orphans

Adoption normally takes place within the joint family, so that use of adoption agencies is relatively rare. A brother and his family will automatically take responsibility for his deceased brother's children as if they were his own. If a mother dies (for example in childbirth) the children *may* be looked after by the mother's parents. (One Punjabi woman informant whose mother died in childbirth was brought up by her mother's sister.) Baby daughters are sometimes adopted within the family. We heard of one case in which a woman's sister-in-law (who had two sons but no daughters) took it for granted that she would adopt one of the woman's twins (not yet born) if they were girls.

Inheritance

Inheritance through the male line is usual, though not universal (e.g. it is through the female line in Kerala). When a father dies, his wealth is shared by his sons, who still belong to the same joint family, though it may be partitioned if the family becomes too large. In theory a girl who marries keeps all the gifts from her family; they act as a kind of insurance, and she can pass them on to her daughters at their marriage.

Birth control and abortion

According to the Sanskrit texts on dharma, a person's ritual life begins at conception, and there is a series of rituals during pregnancy to protect the embryo and its mother. The life of the embryo in the womb is merely one stage in the cycle of rebirth, and some mythical sages were so well prepared by their previous lives that they achieved great wisdom while still in the womb. Some texts hold that all embryos are conscious, and have plenty of time to reflect, in their uncomfortable position, on the miseries of rebirth and the consequences of their past evil *karma*.[7]

Since on this view the embryo is already a living, conscious being, abortion is a great sin, amounting to murder. Further, it is held that the purpose of sexual intercourse is procreation, and that it is a husband's duty to have intercourse with his wife during the fertile part of her menstrual cycle. This would imply that prevention of conception, even by the rhythm method, is forbidden. This, however, is an extreme legalistic view, and is not universal even in the dharma texts. One commentator argues that the rule enjoining intercourse with the wife during her fertile period does not mean that this is compulsory, but only that intercourse at other times, or with another woman, is forbidden. Similarly, although many texts say that intercourse should be solely for the purpose of procreation, it can always be argued that this is a counsel of perfection which cannot be followed in the present fallen age.

Popular attitudes set far less value on the embryo than the dharma texts do. Some women believe that until the fifth month the embryo is a shapeless mass with no personality; on this view, abortion is far less heinous. Traditional midwives in India are reputed to perform abortions, though they are reluctant to admit it. Some Hindus accept abortion on medical grounds, and in this country social influences such as the fragmentation of the joint family may make a woman more likely to opt for abortion.

Great value is set on sons, because of the work they contribute to the family and because property is usually inherited through the male line, as well as because of their place in ritual, the son having the duty of making offerings to the ancestors. Daughters are a liability, because husbands have to be found for them and dowries, or at least expensive weddings, provided. In the past, female infanticide has been practised, though in a furtive way. Now that the sex of a foetus can be discovered through amniocentesis (extracting a sample of the fluid surrounding it), some couples seek to abort female foetuses. This practice has been widely condemned both in India and in the Indian press in Britain, and is certainly not warranted by any Hindu authority. Less drastically, many Hindu wives or husbands undergo sterilization, but not until they have a son, even if they already have several daughters.

Clearly, we cannot give a definite Hindu answer to questions about the control of fertility; we can only indicate the terms in which Hindus are likely to consider them. It is not much discussed between the sexes, even by married couples; matters concerning conception, pregnancy and birth are traditionally the concern of women, who learn about them first from their mothers, and later from the elder women of their husband's families, and from midwives. Nowadays, women health professionals have an important role.

Celibacy and being single

In chapter 1, we introduced the four stages of life that men of the first three varnas pass through according to tradition. These are ideals which influence people, rather than clear stages which many men follow.

The first stage, that of the brahmachārī, involves many forms of austerity, such as sleeping on the ground and not looking in a mirror. Sexual abstinence, however, is the most prominent rule, so that the word brahmacharya, meaning the state of the brahmachārī, has come to mean chastity. This is regarded not simply as self-denial but also as a way of conserving energy; men who practice brahmacharya are believed to be physically and spiritually powerful. The nineteenth-century saint Ramakrishna practised brahmacharya by never consummating his marriage. Gandhi took a vow of brahmacharya when he was already married, as a way of strengthening himself for his non-violent campaigns, and called on his followers to do the same. Some men have avoided marriage, often against the wishes of their families, and become lifelong brahmachārīs.

The fourth stage is that of the sannyāsī, who renounces all ties and no longer performs any ritual; he too abstains from sex. According to the pattern of four stages laid down in the dharma texts, this stage is only entered after married life, and after a preliminary stage of withdrawal from the world as a vānaprastha or forest-dweller; but quite early texts claim that one can become a sannyāsī at any time without going through the other stages. Some sannyāsīs are solitary; others are organised into monastic orders, such as the Rāmakrishna Order, founded in 1897, which young men enter as brahmachārīs, to be later initiated as sannyāsīs.

Some women also have refused marriage and lived a celibate life. Remaining single is traditionally a matter of religious vocation, not secular choice, so that bachelors and spinsters without some kind of religious motive are rare.

21

Notes

1. E. Nesbitt and R. Jackson, 'Growing Up in the Hindu Tradition', *Resource*, 10, 2, Spring, 1988, pp 4-5.

2. W. Menski, 'Legal Pluralism in the Hindu Marriage', in R. Burghart (ed.), *Hinduism in Great Britain* (London, Tavistock Press, 1987).

3. *The Hindu Arranged Marriage* by Mrs. Ramaben Patel and N. Lambert (available from YWCA Blue Triangle Community Centre, Great Central Road, Loughborough, Leicestershire).

4. D.G. Bowen (ed.) *Hinduism in England* (Bradford College, 1981, available from Faculty of Contemporary Studies, Bradford and Ilkley College, Great Horton Road, Bradford, W. Yorkshire).

5. Patel and Lambert (n.3 above), p. 19. See also Amrit Wilson, *Finding a Voice* (London, Virago, 1978), pp 114-116. Although Parminder Bhachu's book *Twice Migrants* (London, Tavistock, 1985) is about Sikhs, Chapter 6 includes useful general information about the dowry system in North India.

6. *A Hindu Wedding* (24 slides with notes). 'People at Worship' series, No. S1526 (The Slide Centre Ltd., Ilton, Ilminster, Somerset, TA19 9HS).

7. W.D. O'Flaherty, *Textual Sources for the Study of Hinduism* (Manchester University Press, 1988), pp 98; 100. See further J.J. Lipner, 'The classical Hindu view on abortion and the moral status of the unborn', in Harold G. Coward, J.J. Lipner and K.K. Young, *Hindu Ethics: Purity, Abortion and Euthanasia*, New York, State University of New York Press, 1989.

8. M. McDonald, 'Rituals of motherhood among Gujarati women in East London', in R. Burghart (ed.), *Hinduism in Great Britain* (London, Tavistock Press, 1987).

3.   Peace, conflict and minority rights

Non-violence and violence

Two key ideas seem to be held in tension within the Hindu tradition. One is *ahimsā* (non-violence, literally 'non-harming') and the other is the righteous use of violence in the pursuit of truth.

The doctrine of non-violence has a long history in India. It was known in the time of the earliest Upanishads (around 700 BCE), where it is included in a list of virtues: 'asceticism, generosity, uprightness, non-violence, speaking the truth'.[1] It is mentioned four times in similar lists in the *Bhagavad-Gītā*.[2] It may have originated as a method by which the ascetic (sannyāsī) seeks to avoid accumulating evil karma. Truth and non-violence are mentioned many times in the *Mahābhārata*, the great epic of ancient India, as general ethical principles, although in particular circumstances, such as warfare, violence is considered legitimate. In the *Bhagavad-Gītā*, which is part of the *Mahābhārata*, Krishna persuades Arjuna to fight because it is his dharma as a warrior.

Non-violence was an important principle for the Buddhists, who flourished in North India from the 5th century BCE. The emperor Ashoka (c. 269-232 BCE), who supported Buddhism, describes in one of his inscriptions how he renounced war as a means of expanding his empire, and resolved to rule by dharma. He also became a vegetarian, and forbade the slaughter of many species of animals.

Non-violence is carried to the greatest lengths by the Jains, who flourished in North India from about the same time as the Buddhists, and are now to be found mainly in Western India. Jains avoid agriculture, because it involves violence to creatures living in the soil; many of them make their living as merchants.

It appears from the earliest texts, the Vedas, that in the second millennium BCE the sacrifice of animals was an approved form of worship. The fact that in most forms of Hindu worship today the offerings are of vegetable produce such as grain, fruit and coconuts, and of milk, curds and ghee (clarified butter), results from the influence of the ideal of non-violence. The Buddhists, and their patron Ashoka, played a large part in promoting this ideal, which is recognised in the Hindu tradition itself. The Buddha is remembered in Hindu mythology as an incarnation of Vishnu, the preserver god, who preached against animal sacrifice out of compassion for animals. Non-violence is especially emphasised by worshippers of Krishna, who is also generally regarded as an incarnation of Vishnu; Krishna worship, like Jainism, flourishes especially in merchant communities, for whom a non-violent ideology is especially congenial. Violence is associated with the worship of some forms of the Mother Goddess, to whom animals are still sometimes sacrificed.

23

As we said above, there is a tension between the ideal of non-violence and the need to defend dharma by force if necessary. Even Ashoka does not seem to have renounced warfare entirely, despite what he says in the inscription mentioned above; for later in the same inscription he threatens forest tribes with death if they resist his rule. The mythology which is remembered by Hindus through storytellers, acting troupes and pictures, and is now available in the form of films, videos and comic strips, abounds in righteous kings who defend dharma by force of arms, and gods who slay demons. The popular autumn festival of Navarātri is associated with two of these stories. In northern and western India it commemorates the righteous king Rāma's defeat and killing of the demon king Rāvana; in Bengal it celebrates the goddess Durgā's killing of the buffalo demon. In historical times, the Maratha king Shivājī (c. 1629-1680), who laid the foundations of a powerful empire in central India, was urged by his guru, the poet Rāmdās, to defend brahmins, the gods, the dharma and the cow. The memory of these and other figures from mythology and history was invoked during the struggle against British rule in the twentieth century.

The doctrine of *ahimsā* was used in modern times by M.K. Gandhi (1869-1948), and through him it became widely known in the West. Gandhi referred to his non-violent struggles aimed at achieving his political ends as *satyāgraha*, literally 'adherence to truth'. *Ahimsā* was the means and truth the objective of his protests. According to Gandhi, all acts of violence are motivated by selfishness. Moreover, if we act violently against fellow human beings, whether by fighting or by way of punishment, we are arrogating to ourselves a right that belongs only to God; for only God knows the rights and wrongs of a case, and can judge who deserves to be punished.

Gandhi's discourse about truth usually revolved around the idea of the *oneness* of things, especially of human beings: the idea of 'the essential unity of God and man and for that matter all that lives',[3] and that 'all mankind in essence are alike'.[4] The belief that human beings are fundamentally different from one another, and that some are inherently superior to others and are thereby entitled to dominate them, is, according to Gandhi, *māyā* – illusion. This is the root of Gandhi's objection to racism in South Africa, to British imperialism, to Hindu-Muslim conflict and to untouchability. It is also an explanation of the changes in his personal life-style towards greater simplicity. He was trying to realize his identity with God by identifying himself with the masses of people who were having their identities denied. This, in turn, became a source of power and charisma in his leadership as the masses began to see him as a man of God. Gandhi is still revered as a great man and a saint, but he has few direct followers in India today. Many younger Hindus see him as a great man of his time and situation, but think that his pacifism is as inappropriate as his anti-industrialism in meeting India's needs in the modern world.

Gandhi was successful in his campaigns of non-violent protest against various British policies; but he was campaigning against British authorities who were sensitive to moral and humanitarian criticism in Britain and the United States. However it should also be noted that Gandhi's advice to the Jews in Nazi Germany was that they should disarm Hitler with their love.

The following anecdotal account records the view of a Punjabi woman of about 30, brought up in Vārānasī (Benares), but now living and working as a policewoman in England. In her opinion few Hindus of her age-group and background would espouse Gandhi's views on pacifism. 'Ahimsā is one value. But defending truth, even if it involves the use of violence, is more important. Wars sometimes have to be fought to uphold peace, as in the *Mahābhārata* and the *Rāmāyana*.' She also pointed out that India has never needed to conscript troops (therefore there is no rule on conscientious objection), and there has been no shortage of volunteers to enlist at time of crisis, at the time of the war with Pakistan or when there have been border disputes with China.

Within some sectarian movements, however, the doctrine of ahimsa is taken very seriously indeed. It is the basis of the Hare Krishna movement's teaching on vegetarianism. Among the five basic human values promulgated by the Sathya Sāi Bābā organization, *ahimsā* is 'the zenith of human achievement and perfection', 'universal love', 'the experience of the essential one-ness of all creation'.

Minority rights

In Hindu society, no community is an overall majority. Rather than a largely homogeneous community in which a number of minorities are encompassed, it presents a multitude of groups differentiated by caste, sect and region. Any of these groups could be called a minority, in the sense that it is far smaller than the total population; but among these minorities some are dominant in the economic, political or ritual spheres, while others have a much smaller share of wealth and power.

The notion of dharma, in which different norms are applicable to different groups of people, provides for a plural society in which each group follows its own way of life without being disturbed by the others, so long as it does not interfere with the privileges or notions of purity of some other group. Often this involves physical separation: different groups live in different parts of the village, so that those who kill and eat animals, for instance, will not pollute the homes of vegetarians. Such arrangements limit social interaction, but they generally operate peacefully provided groups do not infringe each others' privileges. The kind of infringements which lead to trouble may be of clear practical value, as when a caste group attempts to use a well hitherto reserved for higher castes, or takes up a profitable trade which has traditionally been the monopoly of another group; or they may be apparently trivial but of great symbolic value, such as the wearing of a particular style of clothes or shoes.

25

In the sphere of religion, the typical Hindu response to those who do not share one's beliefs is not to oppose them or attempt to convert them but to tolerate them, even if one tolerates them as inferiors. In the *Bhagavad-Gītā*, Krishna, who reveals himself as God incarnate, says:

> Even those who are devoted to other gods and worship them with faith
> are really worshipping Me, though not in the proper way (*BhG* 9, 23).

In this way, Hindus regard the deities worshipped by other sects as subordinate to the one which they worship themselves; or they may regard all deities as different ways of representing the one formless God, each of which is appropriate for certain people, though some may be truer than others. Similarly, those who do not worship images regard those who do so as following a way which suits their level of understanding; those who use only vegetable and milk products in their offerings think that blood sacrifice is a valid form of worship for those who know no better.

Belief in rebirth makes it possible to suppose that all are on their way to salvation, though some have further to go than others. This applies not only to Hindus of different sects, but to those who are not Hindus, such as Christians or Muslims, so long as they do not strive agressively to make converts. What Hindus find hard to accept is any claim to a unique revelation or a single path to salvation.

Historically, Hinduism has been hospitable to non-Hindu religious minorities. Already in the first few centuries CE, there were communities of Jews and Christians on the south-west coast of India, enjoying privileges granted them by Hindu kings. From the eighth century, there have been communities of Muslims, and of Zoroastrians from Iran, who are known in India as Parsis. Hindu rulers have generally protected religious minorities; Shivājī, whom we mentioned above as a champion of Hinduism, respected Christian friars as well as Muslims during his wars of conquest, and returned mosques and copies of the Qur'an into Muslim hands.

Modern India is a secular state, in which discrimination on religious grounds is unlawful. Where strife has occurred between Hindus and Muslims, Sikhs or other religious minorities, it has arisen from a perceived conflict of political or economic interests, and not primarily from religious differences. Nevertheless, such conflicts are among the greatest problems facing India today.

The most burning minority rights issue in the Hindu tradition is that of untouchability.[5] In 1917 the Indian National Congress, in response to a call from a meeting of Untouchables in Bombay, urged the removal of 'all disabilities imposed by custom on the Depressed Classes' (the current official term for Untouchables). For the next thirty years the position of the Untouchables was the second most contentious communal problem in India, next to that of the Muslims. Electoral arrangements providing positive discrimination in favour of them were included in the Government of India Act of 1919, and further provision was made in the Government of India Act of 1935. As early as 1878 they were given positive discrimination in education through concessions in fees. But such provisions did not prevent the exclusion of Untouchables from public facilities such as roads and wells, and in some respects the legal system of British India reinforced discrimination in an attempt to avoid interfering with Indian custom.

Gandhi's work on behalf of Untouchables is well known, but his opposition to separate electoral arrangements for them, and his refusal to regard them as a separate community, were bitterly resented, especially by the Untouchable leader Dr. B.R. Ambedkar. It was Gandhi who gave them the name *Harijans*, 'children of God', but this name is often used pejoratively, and is rejected by many Untouchables as a legacy of Gandhi's paternalistic attitude. Untouchables today often use the term *Dalit*, 'oppressed', of themselves, and in South India the title *Ādi Drāvida*, 'original Dravidians'.[6]

The Republican Constitution of 1950 abolished the practice of untouchability 'forthwith', and the Indian Parliament passed the Untouchability (Offences) Act 1955 – a comprehensive law making it an offence to impose 'disabilities on the ground of untouchability' in matters such as access to temples, public transport, education and water supplies. The law is not effectively enforced, however; only about 500 cases of discrimination get as far as the courts each year, and in 1976, for example, there were only about 70 convictions. The 1971 census showed the Untouchable literacy rate to be half the national average of 30%. Untouchables comprise about 15% of the Indian population. On the basis of the 1971 population figures this would give a total of at least 84 million (4 times the number of blacks in the USA at that time).[7]

One cannot emphasise too much that many Hindus are opposed to untouchability. But the phenomenon is nevertheless very real. The situation for most Untouchables is as bad as ever. Official Indian figures suggest that there are routinely more than 10,000 violent attacks on Untouchables in a year. The real figure is probably much higher.

Fifty-three per cent of villages sampled in a recent survey still denied the right to use common village wells to anyone from Untouchable castes, while 71 per cent of the villagers barred these (Hindu) castes from the local Hindu temple. The economic deprivation of Untouchables often takes the form of debt-bondage, a form of semi-slavery in which workers are bound to their masters until debts can be paid off.

The backlash against positive discrimination towards Untouchables is exemplified by a rebellion by medical students in Gujarat against government attempts to reserve medical school places for Untouchables.

27

Dalits are not a mute and passive group. The anger felt by many Dalits comes across vividly when the poet Keshav Meshram writes:

On my birthday, I cursed God.
I cursed him, I cursed him again.
Whipping him with words, I said
'Bastard!'
'Would you chop a whole cart full of wood for a single piece of bread?'[8]

Dalits also assert themselves through organisations. The Dalit Liberation Education Trust is based in Madras and, under the directorship of Henry Thiagaraj (himself a Dalit), the Trust's Education Facilitation Centre runs various projects for Untouchables in the state of Tamil Nadu. These include residential camps for young, unemployed Dalits in their late teens or early twenties, and various village-based projects. The camps include confidence-building exercises and training in inter-personal communication. Use is made of role play, street theatre and informal social activities in encouraging students to improve their image of their own abilities and potential. One rural development project includes the following as its aims:

To educate and conscientise the landless, small and marginal
farmers of Dalit communities.
To create awareness and bring local leadership.
To educate people to become critically aware of their problems
and motivate them to solve the same.

One example observed by one of the authors in 1988 was based in a group of villages near Mahabalipuram. A meeting of 'animators', young men and women from Dalit castes recruited from the villages and trained by the project's rural development officer – another Dalit skilled in street theatre – was observed. There were role play exercises in which young women practised tackling a male official who was not interested in listening to their case, and oral reports from the animators of their experiences in the villages. The emphasis was on self-help and the building of self-confidence.

These initiatives are splendid, but prejudice against Untouchables in Indian society runs very deep. One traditional way of avoiding untouchability is by changing religion, as many did in following Dr. Ambedkar in 1956 into conversion to Buddhism. Many others have converted to Christianity and Islam, and more recently to Bahá'ism.

Untouchability is a deeply entrenched part of the Indian social system, however, and the change of religion does not imply a change of status. Indeed, the latest video produced by the Education Facilitation Centre is called *The Twice Discriminated*, and shows how Dalit Christians lose out twice: first by being untouchable and second by being Christian and therefore ineligible for the benefits which result from the Government's positive discrimination towards Hindu Untouchables. The video also documents the marginalisation of Dalit Christians *within* the Church, illustrating that caste discrimination extends beyond Hinduism.[9]

Notes

1. *Chhāndogya Upanishad* 3, 17, 4.

2. *BhG* 10, 5; 13, 7; 16, 2; 17, 4.

3. Gandhi in *Young India*, December 1924.

4. Gandhi in *Harijan*, November 1938.

5. The term 'untouchable' and its relation to ritual impurity is discussed in Jackson and Killingley, *Approaches to Hinduism*, pp 81-2.

6. 'Dravidian' is the name of the family of languages most commonly spoken in South India.

7. *The Untouchables of India*, Report No 26, Minority Rights Group, 1982 (from M.R.G., 29 Craven Street, London, WC2N 5NT).

8. Barbara Joshi (ed.), *Untouchable! Voices of the Dalit Liberation Movement* (London, Zed Books and the Minority Rights Group, 1986). Data in the previous three paragraphs are from the same book.

9. Available from The Education Facilitation Centre, 161 T.T.K. Salai, Alwarpet, Madras 18, India.

4. Humankind and nature

Reverence for life

If we define life in purely physical terms, we may think of it as the capacity to grow, to adapt to changes in the environment, and to reproduce. But Hindus see life as more than this. Each living thing has a conscious self. In lower animals this self is less able to express itself than in human beings, just as among people there are some who are more fully and clearly conscious than others. Many Hindus believe that plants have life in this sense, and one of the most original modern Hindu scientists, the biologist and physicist J C Bose (1858-1937), sought to show through experiments that plants are conscious of themselves.

Life, then, is essentially the same in all living beings, although as human beings we have more control over our actions, and consequently over our destiny, than animals or plants have, and we are capable of self-fulfilment and liberation. The texts of Hinduism written in Sanskrit often refer to a scale of living beings 'from Brahmā down to a tuft of grass' – that is, from the highest of the gods to the simplest plant. Human beings are somewhere near the top of this scale, but not at the top, because above them are various ranks of demigods and gods. Moreover, if we are human now, that does not mean we are human for ever. We are going to die, and after that we are going to be reborn: possibly in human form, but possibly also in some higher form of life, or in a lower form, depending on the good and evil deeds we have done. This process of rebirth is described graphically in the *Bhagavad-Gītā*.

> Just as in this body the embodied self has childhood, youth and old age, in the same way it gets another body; the wise man is not confused about that (*BhG* 2, 13).

> Just as a man abandons his old clothes and puts on new ones, the embodied self abandons its old bodies and goes to new ones (*BhG* 2, 22).

The idea of rebirth links all living beings in one fellowship, so that harming anything living, not only a person, can be thought of as an injury to a fellow-being. Moreover, many Hindu texts say that all living beings are different forms of one being, or that God is present in all of them; we should therefore have equal respect or all beings, whether ourselves or others, high or low born, animal or human.

> On a brahmin full of knowledge and good conduct, on a cow, or on an elephant, on a dog, or on a person of unclean caste, wise men look with equal eye (*BhG* 5, 18).

While the body changes all the time and perishes at death, the true self never changes or dies, and is not marked by differences of character, sex, caste or species. If we value ourselves above the beings around us, and seek to preserve or gratify our bodies at the expense of the suffering of other beings, we are falling into the error of identifying ourselves with our bodies, and not with the unchanging self, and this error condems us to continued rebirth. We thus injure ourselves as well as setting enmity between ourselves and God who is present in all beings. Chapter 16 of the *Bhagavad-Gītā* describes this error in detail.

> Selfishness, force, pride and anger are their ways. It is God, in their own and others' bodies, that they hate in their resentment (*BhG* 16, 18).

If, on the other hand, we know that the self in all beings is the same, or that God is present in all, we will not harm other beings, and thus will not condemn ourselves to rebirth.

> The supreme God dwells in all beings equally, and does not perish when they perish; he who sees this, truly sees.

> For, seeing that the Lord dwells everywhere equally, he does not injure himself by himself, and goes to the highest place (*BhG* 13, 27-8).

Abstention from injury to all beings is an important ideal in Hinduism. This ideal, known as *ahimsā* or non-violence, is discussed in Chapter 3, pp. 23-25.

The fact that non-violence is a Hindu ideal does not mean that Hindus never fight, kill animals or eat meat. Hindu ethical teachers recognize that ideals cannot always be put into practice by everyone, and while non-violence is taught as a guiding principle for all, it is most often laid down as a practice for ascetics – people making a special effort to pursue the holy life and to escape from the cycle of rebirth. Injury to animals is thought of as bringing guilt, and thus leading to misfortune of all kinds including rebirth in low forms; but rebirth brings with it a propensity to continue in sinful actions, and we cannot all escape the cycle at once.

Reverence for life is expressed in the offerings which Hindus often make to wild animals and birds. In the *Bhāgavata Purāna*, a popular Sanskrit text dating from about the tenth century CE, the ideal householder is exhorted to share his food with all living beings:

> A householder should regard deer, camels, donkeys, mice, snakes, birds and bees as his sons; for what difference is there between his sons and them? (*BhP* 7, 14, 9).

Particular kinds of plants and animals are regarded as sacred. The tulsī or basil plant is sacred to Vishnu, and the bilva or bel to Shiva; devotees of these gods cultivate the plants and use their leaves in worship. The peepul or sacred fig tree has been worshipped from ancient times, and Hindus avoid cutting down one of these trees while it is living.

Monkeys are often treated as sacred; they are all relatives of the monkey god Hanuman, who was a friend of Rāma. Snakes are often regarded as guardians of the pieces of land they live in, to be propitiated by the people who till the soil there. Bowls of milk are left for them. Stones carved with snakes are a common form of open-air shrine. Snakes have a festival of their own, Nāga-Panchamī ('the snakes' fifth', the fifth day of the dark half of the lunar month Shrāvana); it falls in July or August, around the beginning of the rainy season, when snakes abound in India. If someone is bitten by a snake, people may think that this is because the person has failed to worship snakes. The god Shiva wears a snake around his neck, and the eternal snake Shesha or Ananta forms the couch of Vishnu.

Above all, cattle are revered by Hindus, and killing them is considered an even graver sin than killing other animals. This reverence is an expression of gratitude for their usefulness; not only does the cow give milk, but the bullock is essential in India for drawing carts and ploughs, while dung is valued both as manure and as a fuel, and also for plastering floors. The bull is the animal on which Shiva rides, and bulls are often dedicated to temples of Shiva as an act of piety or in fulfilment of a vow. Such bulls are allowed to wander and graze freely. Cattle are not so ubiquitous in this country as in India, but British Hindus still express their reverence for them by refusing to eat beef.

Attitudes to the environment[1]

The Hindu tradition is well aware of the way in which human beings depend on their environment, and many Hindus live in close contact with the soil. The attitude to cattle is an example of this awareness; for they provide us with food, not only through milk, butter and curds (yoghurt), but through the labour of bullocks in the fields. The reverence and protection which Hindus feel they owe to cattle is an expression of gratitude for the bounty of the earth.

Religious acts are a way of repaying what we owe to the environment. This is made plain in the *Bhagavad-Gītā*, chapter 3, which describes worship as a way of repaying the gods:

> For the gods, prospered by worship, will give the food you wish for; whoever enjoys their gifts without giving them, is nothing but a thief (*BhG* 3, 12).

Worship does not necessarily consist of ritual acts; later the *Bhagavad-Gītā* tells us that all our actions can be offered in worship to God (BhG 9, 27).

The *Laws of Manu*, a collection of verses on ritual and other duties, especially of Brahmins, dating from the second century CE, gives a more formal view of how we are to repay our debt to the environment. Manu refers to the ways in which daily life involves us in the bondage of sin, through the injury and destruction we inflict on living beings, including the seeds we crush for food and the microscopic organisms in our drinking water. He then prescribes ways of expiating this sin.

33

A householder has five slaughterhouses : the hearth, the millstone, the broom, the mortar, and the water jar; by using these he is bound.

To expiate each of these in turn, the great sages devised five great daily acts of worship for householders.

Study of the Veda is the worship of Brahman; offerings of water are the worship of the ancestors; offerings in fire are for the gods, the scattering of food is for the spirits, and service to guests is the worship of man (*Manu* 3, 68-70).

These daily duties are thus regarded as compensating for the damage we do by living.

Our dependence on the environment is also expressed in the festivals of Hinduism. The Tamils of South India celebrate a three-day festival called Pongal, at the winter solstice. On the first day, Indra, the god of rain, is worshipped. On the second day, rice boiled in milk is offered to the sun as it begins its northward journey from the Tropic of Capricorn to the Tropic of Cancer. This is the main day, from which the festival takes its name; *pongal* in Tamil means "it has boiled". On the third day, cattle are washed and garlanded, and are given some of the boiled rice, together with sweets. They are not put to work, but allowed to wander about wearing their garlands. The festival thus shows the people's gratitude to three things on which they depended for their food: rain and sun to nourish the rice crop, and cattle to provide milk and work in the fields.

Rivers, which provide the water for drinking, washing, irrigation and many other uses, are sacred for Hindus, and are regarded as a gift of the gods. The greatest of them is Gangā, the Ganges, which flows through northern India; but there is also a heavenly Gangā which is the source of this and all other rivers. Gangā is regarded as a goddess, and so is the earth; the female is associated in Hindu thought with fertility and the provision of food. Many Hindus pray to the earth for forgiveness before touching it with their feet when they get up on the morning, since to touch someone with your foot is disrespectful. The earth is also worshipped before starting to build a house or temple, as compensation for the violence that will be done to it, and purified so as to provide an auspicious site.

The whole world is a manifestation of God. This is shown dramatically in Chapter 11 of the *Bhagavad-Gītā*, where Krishna tells Arjuna:

See the whole world with its moving and unmoving beings in one place here today, in my body, Arjuna; and whatever else you wish to see (*BhG* 11, 7).

This idea is very old, since we find it in a Vedic hymn composed around 1,000 BCE. The divine source of the universe is there called Purusha, 'Man'; but we might translate the word as 'God', and indeed that is how the hymn is usually understood:

Purusha is all this, which has been and is to be, and the Lord of Immortality, and what grows by food (*Rig-Veda* 10, 90, 2).[2]

One of Gandhi's favourite texts was the begining of the *Ishā Upanishad*:

The universe, whatever moves in the world, is to be dwelt in by God. Enjoy it by renouncing it; do not covet anyone's wealth.

This means that the right way to enjoy the world is not to regard any part of it as your own, or as something you wish was your own, but to recognise that it belongs to God.

Work and leisure

Most Hindus, living in India's villages, are well aware of the necessity of work to gain a livelihood from the earth. People's aims in this world are often summed up in Hindu texts as these three: pleasure (kama), profit (artha), and righteousness (dharma). These are described in Chapter 1 (p. 9). This view of the three worldly aims allows a place for leisure and pleasure as well as for work and the fulfilment of duties.

Play is essential to the life of the universe. God himself creates the universe by playing; for since God by definition has no needs, there is no other explanation for his actions. The great seventh-century theologian Shankara gives an analogy:

In this world princes and other exalted men, who have no desires left unfulfilled, act with no motivation, but merely for fun, in places of recreation and so on ... Similarly, God's activity could be merely for fun, arising out of his own nature
(Shankara on *Vedānta-Sūtra* 2, 1, 33).

The idea of play is apparent especially in the mythology of Krishna, the playful form of the god Vishnu. In festivals connected with Krishna, especially Holī and Janmāshtamī (Krishna's birthday), his devotees imitate him by having as much fun as they can.

The fact that salvation (moksha) is the ultimate value does not mean that Hindus are necessarily unconcerned with this world. Many Hindu communities have traditions of hard work and set great value on worldly success – this is especially evident among peasant and trading castes, from which many of the Punjabi and Gujarati Hindus in Britain have come. Among Gujarati Vaishnavas of the Pushti Mārga (Vallabha) and Swāminārāyan traditions, worldly success is counted as evidence of God's favour.

On the other hand, people who despise worldly values are highly regarded. A passage in the *Bhāgavata Purāna* describes an ascetic who makes no effort to maintain himself, but takes whatever food, clothing and shelter happen to come to him; sometimes he fares well and sometimes badly, but it makes no difference to him. Preaching about the vanity of worldly desires and efforts, he uses the bee as an example – not to show the value of hard work and forethought, but to show their worthlessness:

> I have learnt to be indifferent to all desires from the example of the bee: when a man has laboriously gathered wealth, another may kill the owner and take it from him, like honey from the bee (*BhP* 7, 13, 35).

This contemptuous attitude to work is associated with the idea that *karma* – deeds, actions or work – binds us to worldly existence, causing us to be reborn in new forms in which we reap the fruits of our previous actions. To escape from rebirth, it would seem to be necessary to abstain from activity altogether.

But many teachers include work as part of the way to salvation. The *Bhagavad-Gītā* points out that it is impossible to live without activity:

> Do the action that is required of you; action is better than inaction. And even the functioning of the body would not succeed without action (*BhG* 3, 8).

The next verse says that action for the purpose of worship, unlike all other action, does not bind us to rebirth. We have seen that the *Bhagavad-Gītā* regards such action as a way of repaying what we take from the environment.

Gandhi developed his own interpretation of this doctrine, saying that in this chapter of the *Bhagavad-Gītā* worship means 'body-labour for service'. He believed that we all owe a debt of manual labour to the world, to repay what we eat. This idea, which he also calls 'bread-labour', he took from Tolstoy, but it touched a chord among Hindu peasants, for whom real work means tilling the ground, not trading or working in an office.

Bodily health

Purity and the avoidance of pollution are key ideas in Hindu practice, though Hindu ideas of purity do not always correspond to modern ideas of hygiene. Great care is taken in bodily cleanliness, and daily bathing is common. Hindus traditionally wash in a river, or in a large (artifical) pool called a tank. In a modern house, a shower is much better than a bath, because the head, which it is most important to keep pure, will not be polluted by water that has bathed the feet, which are constantly exposed to pollution. Most Hindus remove their shoes before entering a house, or else before entering some part of the house such as the kitchen or the upper floor. Incense is often burnt to purify the air and make it pleasant, especially where the gods are worshipped.

Insistence on purity applies particularly to food and drink. Firstly, these must be of the right kind; everyone avoids unclean food, though ideas of what is unclean vary between regions and castes. But they must also not have become polluted on their way to the person who consumes them. Hindus are careful to wash their hands before and after meals, and before entering the kitchen. Food and drink can become polluted through contact with the mouth; for this reason Hindus eat chapatis (Indian bread) by tearing bits off with their fingers, not by biting them. This is done with the right hand, the left being used for unclean purposes. Many Hindus are able to drink by pouring from a cup or glass without touching it with their lips. Further, left-over food is unclean; some Hindus are so particular about this that if they have been interrupted in a meal they will throw the food away.

Food is an important factor in marking a caste as high or low. The eating of meat is generally a mark of low caste, though not invariably. Bengali brahmins eat fish, and are looked down on for this reason by Hindus of other regions. It is often held that castes with fighting traditions need to eat meat, usually mutton or goat, but also sometimes wild pig, which they hunt. Domestic pigs and poultry are unclean, while only the lowest, untouchable castes eat beef, because of the sanctity of the cow.

Different castes have different traditional rules as to whom they accept food from. While raw food can be received from the hands of the people who grow it, or anyone else, even if they are of lower caste than the eater, cooked food is more susceptible to pollution, and is generally accepted only from people of the same or a higher caste. This makes for complicated arrangements on such occasions as village weddings: a wealthy peasant, for instance, may be expected to provide a feast for the whole village, but will be careful to seat low-caste people at a distance from the rest, and to engage a brahmin to cook for the brahmins. If a brahmin household employs a cook, he is usually a brahmin, and tea-shops and restaurants in India are often run by brahmins, because everyone will accept food and drink from them. Practice is much freer in cities than in villages, and freer again outside India; but British Hindus often observe rules such as not wearing outdoor shoes in the kitchen, or not handling food with the left hand, and they are usually particular about not eating beef, or in many cases any meat, fish or food containing egg or animal fat.

Modern practices such as the sale of ready-cooked or prepared foods, and women having full working and social lives outside the home, make it difficult to keep up traditional food habits all the time. This makes the occasional eating of traditional food, prepared in traditional ways, an important way of asserting traditional values for British Hindus. At the temple after Sunday worship, or at a wedding feast, food that has been cooked with great care from traditional ingredients, some of them imported from India, is enjoyed for the sense of occasion as well as for its varied, subtle and evocative flavours. Eating together is also an assertion of fellowship, cutting across caste boundaries.

Vegetarianism is part of the Hindu respect of life, and connected with the idea of rebirth. Manu says:

> For every hair on the body of a beast, the person who kills it without reason will be slaughtered in successive births (*Manu* 5, 38).

Eggs are avoided by many Hindus, since even if they are unfertilized they are potentially living. Some Hindus do not eat red vegetables such as tomatoes or beetroot, to avoid even seeming to eat food stained with blood.

Not all Hindus are vegetarians, but many Hindus in Britain are, especially those from Gujarati trading castes which value non-violence highly. Among the Hindu movements which have attracted Western disciples, vegetarianism is taken particularly seriously by the International Society for Krishna Consciousness (The Hare Krishna Movement).[3] Its founder A.C. Bhaktivedanta Swami, who went to the United States to preach Krishna worship in 1965, delighted his American followers by telling them that for every chicken that had been fried in his famous Kentucky recipe, Colonel Saunders would be reborn as a chicken.

Many Hindus, however, regard vegetarianism as a counsel of perfection which they do not practise themselves, though they respect those who follow it. Manu sums up their attitude:

> Meat-eating is not wrong, nor alcohol, nor sex. These are natural actions of living beings; but abstention from such action is highly rewarded (*Manu* 5, 56).

The first part of this verse may seem shocking to those Hindus who abstain from meat and alcohol, but the last part shows that such abstinence is highly valued. This is an example of the way Hindu answers to moral questions are often in relative terms, judging an action to be better or less good, not in terms of absolute right and wrong.

Many Hindus take vows to abstain periodically from meat or other foods that they eat the rest of the time. Some people abstain from particular foods on particular days of the week or the lunar month. Fasting, partial or complete, is often undertaken by women for the benefit of their husbands or families, since any form of abstention is held to bring merit; it is also undertaken by men.

Hindus are generally strict about drink and drugs, though this also varies with different groups. Cannabis and alcohol are used in Tantric ritual, which seeks to gain freedom from the restrictions of worldly existence through systematic breaking of the rules which govern ordinary Hindu life. Such practices are restricted to initiates. Individuals and groups who regularly use alcohol or other drugs are usually looked down on by others. Hindu views in such matters are relativistic, as the above verse from Manu shows.

Use of natural resources

It is now widely recognised by ecologists that vegetarianism is a far more economical way of using land than raising animals for meat. Hindu eating habits thus make fewer demands on natural resources than the usual Western ones. On the other hand, there is a very grave threat to the ecology of India from the demand for fuel for domestic fires: forests are reduced, and cowdung is also burnt which would otherwise have manured the ground. This is not strictly a religious problem, but the decline of natural resources is a recurrent theme in Sanskrit religious literature. It is a feature of the age in which we live – the Kali age, the fourth and last in the cycle of ages of the world (p. 2). The Kali age began in 3,102 BCE, and will continue for thousands of centuries. In this age, the Purānas say:

> People will always be anxious, emaciated by scarcity in a land without food, and terrified of drought (*BhP* 12, 3 39).

Descriptions of the Kali age usually link this misery with the wickedness of rulers and people in this age, suggesting that we get the kind of world we deserve as a result of our karma.

The Hindu tradition encourages its followers to treat their environment with respect. The cow is revered as a representative of the whole of nature, and – since God is present in the whole world – as a manifestation of divinity.

Attitudes to the environment are partly governed by the Hindu ideal of non-violence (ahimsā) described in Chapter 3, and by the idea that the individual soul can be reborn as an animal or plant. Non-violence is not restricted to vegetarianism; all agriculture is to some extent a violation of the natural world. The ground is full of living beings, some too small to see, and the farmer is constantly crushing them with his spade or plough. Brahmins traditionally do not till the ground, to avoid committing violence; even if they own land, they let it out to tenant farmers. Not all brahmins follow this rule, but its existence as an ideal shows that agriculture is regarded as a relatively sinful, though necessary, way of life.

This is one reason why the man who has renounced the world, the sannyāsī, is respected. Having cut himself off from all social structures, he lives on wild plants, taking only what nature has provided and not what has been grown by tilling the soil. He thus interferes as little as possible with his environment, and separates himself from the economic system which depends on the exploitation of nature.

But it has never been taught that all Hindus should become sannyāsīs. For those who have not renounced society, it is a virtuous act to adapt the environment for the benefit of other beings – for instance, by digging wells and planting shade trees, which are often mentioned in Sanskrit literature as praiseworthy actions of kings and other wealthy men. The *Bhagavad-Gītā* teaches that the wise man should not attempt to cease acting, but should act for the maintenance of the world:

> Just as the unenlightened act with attachment, so also should the enlightened person act, but without attachment, seeking to maintain the world (*BhG* 3, 25; cf 5, 25).

Those who abstain from harming the environment may also protect it from the violence of others. Hindu holy men have a protective attitude to all living beings, and there are many stories in Hindu mythology of forest hermits who shelter wild animals from predators and hunters.

Concern for natural resources may bring people into conflict with powerful outside interests. The Chipko movement was established in 1973 to resist deforestation throughout Nepal and the Himalayan foothills. Overcropping trees for the timber industry and for fuel causes erosion of top soil. The consequent damage to farming prompts migration to the plains, which are already densely populated, besides the silting and flooding caused by erosion of soil into the rivers. The Chipko movement uses a form of non-violent struggle; people link hands round the trees to prevent them from being felled. The movement looks back to an incident in 1730, when tribal women in Rajasthan embraced trees to prevent them being felled for fuel for the Maharaja of Jodhpur's lime kilns; the women gave their lives, for they were cut down together with the trees. Their prayer was:

> You guard us, you feed us, you give us the breath of life.
> Tree, give me your strength to protect you.

Animal rights

To speak of animals, or indeed people, as having rights is perhaps too legalistic in a Hindu context. Rather, we should speak of the relative moral goodness of actions which benefit or spare animals, and the relative badness of actions which harm them.

We have already seen that the world of living beings includes not only people but animals and even plants. While complete abstention from harm is impossible, cruelty is definitely sinful, whether to people or animals, and kindness to any being is meritorious. There are many stories of acts of kindness to animals; the most outstanding hero of this kind is King Shibi, who gave his own flesh to a hawk in order to spare the life of a dove.[4] His kindness was not only to the dove but to the hawk as well.

Peasants, the people who have most to do with animals, are aware of the value of their own beasts, and avoid harming or neglecting them. They may even look on a cow as a respected member of the family, and give it special food and decorate it at festivals. On the other hand, they have their own interests to think of, and are not always averse to selling a worn-out beast to a non-Hindu trader, usually a Muslim, without asking questions about what happens once it has left their hands. One can avoid doing harm oneself, but cannot always prevent others doing it.

There is an instructive passage in the *Mahābhārata* whose attitudes many Hindus today would agree with. A brahmin in search of a great moral teacher is directed to a hunter. The brahmin is puzzled that a man who follows a cruel trade should be a moralist, so the hunter explains:

> Undoubtedly I practise cruel deeds, but fate is powerful and previous karma is hard to escape (*MBh* 3, 199, 1-2).

Later he tells how he was once a brahmin himself, but was cursed to be reborn as a hunter when he accidentally wounded a sage with an arrow. He is now living out the effects of his evil deed by following a cruel way of life, though he hurts animals as little as he can. He points out that total non-violence is impossible, not only for himself but for anyone else:

> In the old days, men said amazed: 'Non-violence!' But who does not harm living beings in this world? All things considered, no-one in this world is non-violent.

> Sages who delight in non-violence do violence too – though very little, because they are careful (*MBh* 3, 199, 28-9).

He gives examples to show how violence is essential to life:

> Creatures live on creatures, many times over; living beings eat one another. What do you think of that?

> Men kill many creatures that live in the earth with their feet when they walk. What do you think of that? (*MBh* 3, 199, 24-5).

He even uses the example of King Shibi, to show that flesh-eating has its place; Shibi, after all, was encouraging this practice by giving his own flesh to the hawk.

Hindus are aware of the damage we do to our environment by living in it, even if we are vegetarian. Many Hindus work on the land; some are involved in experiments on animals. The attitude of the hunter in the *Mahābhārata* story shows how we can approach such problems through the relativistic moral attitude of Hinduism. We cannot avoid harming living beings; we know it is sinful, but we are born in a sinful age, as a result of our own previous sins. We still have the choice, however, of harming beings no more than we find necessary, and not being cruel for pleasure. We can also extend our love to all beings, from Brahmā to a tuft of grass, and recognize them as manifestations of God, however imperfect.

Notes

1. For a modern Hindu discussion see O.P. Dwivedi and B.N. Tiwari, *Environmental Crisis and Hindu religion* (Delhi, Gitanjali Publishing House, 1987).

2. For the whole hymn see R.C. Zaehner, *Hindu Scriptures*, pp 8-10; W. O'Flaherty, *The Rig Veda*, pp 30f; W. O'Flaherty, *Textual Sources for the Study of Hinduism* (Manchester University Press, 1988), pp 27f.

3. See Adiraja dasa, *The Hare Krishna Book of Vegetarian Cookery* (Letchmore Heath, Bhaktivedanta Book Trust, 1984).

4. Retold in D. Killingley (ed.), *A Handbook of Hinduism for Teachers* (Newcastle upon Tyne, Grevatt & Grevatt, 1984), pp 9f.

The Authors

Robert Jackson is Reader in Arts Education at the University of Warwick. His recent publications include *Approaches to Hinduism* (John Murray 1988) written with Dermot Killingley, *Religions Through Festivals: Hinduism* (Longman 1989), *Listening to Hindus* (Unwin Hyman 1990) written with Eleanor Nesbitt, and *The Junior RE Handbook* (Stanley Thornes 1990), edited with Dennis Starkings.

Dermot Killingley is Senior Lecturer in Religious Studies at the University of Newcastle upon Tyne. His publications include *The Only True God: Works on Religion by Rammohun Roy,* and *A Handbook of Hinduism for Teachers* which he edited (both published by Grevatt and Grevatt). He wrote *Approaches to Hinduism* (John Murray 1988) with Robert Jackson, and with Siew-Yue Killingley edited *Farewell the Plumed Troop: A Memoir of the Indian Cavalry 1919-1945,* by D.M. Killingley (Grevatt and Grevatt 1990).